HOW TO MANAGE
YOUR MONEY

HOW TO MANAGE YOUR MONEY

by
Larry Burkett

Illustrations by Joe Ragont

MOODY PRESS
CHICAGO

© 1975 by
CHRISTIAN FINANCIAL CONCEPTS
Moody Press Revised Edition, 1982

Library of Congress Cataloging in Publication Data

Burkett, Larry.
  How to manage your money.

  1. Finance, Personal—Religious aspects—
Christianity. I. Title.
HG179.B837   1982   332.024   82-7904
ISBN 0-8024-2547-X   AACR2

21 22 Printing/VI/Year 90 89 88 87

Printed in the United States of America

CONTENTS

SECTION   PAGE

Introduction   7
How to Use This Study   8

1. What Is Wealth?   9
   God's Definition of Wealth
   The Christian's Wealth

2. God's Will in Finances   15
   Stewardship
   God's Wisdom in Money

3. The Perils of Money   23
   Servitude to Money
   Conditions of Servitude

4. Release from Servitude   35
   Freedom from Worry

5. Financial Planning—God's Way (Part 1)   45
   What Is Planning?
   Steps to Short-Range Plans

6. Financial Planning—God's Way (Part 2)   53
   Establishing Long-Range Plans

7. Motives for Accumulating Wealth   63
   God's Attitude
   Why People Accumulate Money

8. How Much Is Enough?   73
   Living Expenses, Investments, Retirement, and Inheritance

9. Sharing by God's Plan   81
   The Tithe—Is It Applicable?
   Sharing from Obedience, Abundance, Sacrifice

10. Who Deserves Help?   93
    Don't Help Everyone—Giving to the Family
    Giving to the Shepherds, the Body, and the Unsaved

11. God's Principles of Financial Decisions   103
    Financial Breathing
    Applying God's Wisdom

12. Practical Applications   113
    Personal Communications Goals and Marriage Goals
    Family Goals

Introduction

This study is provided to help Christians understand God's attitude about *wealth*. There is so much religious "folklore" in the financial realm that few Christians understand what is from God's Word and what is not.

Having taught this subject in many Bible studies, I know what a revelation it is for most Christians to discover how much God does care about money.

There are approximately 700 direct references to money in the Bible and hundreds more indirect references. Nearly two-thirds of all the parables Christ left us deal with the use of *money*. You will discover, as you progress through this study, that God equates our use of wealth with our commitment to Him.

I hope that as a result of this study you will experience absolute peace in the area of finances, for that is what God promises. Do not wait until you finish the entire study to apply God's principles. As you recognize a need, apply God's cure. Share these principles with others and discuss them freely.

Too long we have pretended that Christians have no financial problems. That is nonsense. We are subject to the same temptations as the nonbeliever. It is only through God's blessing that we can escape from those snares. But how can we experience His blessing if we don't understand His plan? We cannot; therefore, this study will focus on God's plan exclusively.

Remember, these are God's principles—not His laws. He will not punish anyone for violations. Those who fail will simply not receive His blessings in the area of finances and will suffer along with the nonbeliever. Most of the rewards promised in Scripture are predicated on our obedience to these principles. Therefore, to achieve these rewards, we must understand and follow God's plan.

I find many Christians have lived by these principles all their lives, but never understood the scriptural basis. Therefore, they were never able to transfer their knowledge to others. This study will help you share these concepts on a scripturally sound basis.

For further information contact: Christian Financial Concepts, Route 4 Hidden Lake, Dahlonega, Georgia 30533.

How to Use This Study

This material is planned to be used in group discussion studies where possible. The scriptural principles are presented from God's Word, and writing space is provided for individual analysis.

Read the Scripture as referenced, write your own analysis, and prepare to share your insight with others in your group.

There is no time requirement for each section. Proceed as quickly or as slowly as your group decides, but stick to a regular routine (such as one section per week). Many of the areas of this study are thought-provoking and controversial, and if you tie up an entire study period on one issue, it will be difficult to finish the entire plan. It is often preferable to prepare and evaluate a section before opening the discussion to questions.

1
What Is Wealth?

"Thou dost make him to rule over the works of thy hands; thou hast put all things under his feet" *(Psalm 8:6).*

What Is Wealth?

God's Definition of Wealth

Do you equate money with wealth? What about other possessions such as cars, houses, or clothes?

Have you ever wondered why God makes us work on this earth? Why doesn't He simply supply our needs as He did Adam and Eve?

1. Read Genesis 3:19. What does it mean to you?

Historically, wealth has been related to ownership—land, camels, cattle, slaves. Currently, wealth is often expressed in representational ideas. For example, the dollar has no objective value (as an item) but it stands for ownership. Similarly, the value of a stock is not based on the value of the company, but on the collective opinion of the public about the stock. Even gold, which has fascinated man through the ages, has a value based on opinion—as illustrated by sharp speculative increases and decreases.

Wealth is also related to our *creative ability* and our *credit* or *borrowing ability*—the trust others have in us. Thus, wealth becomes *an extension of our personalities.* According to our personality, it can be used creatively—spreading the gospel and building hospitals and churches, or it can be wasted—spending it on frivolous activities. It can be corruptive—using it to purchase influence, or it can be destructive—buying guns and bombs. Wealth is what God entrusts to us.

God's Wealth. What is the basic difference between the resource supplied by God and that delivered by the world?

2. Read Proverbs 10:22 and explain how it applies to our lives.

_____

Our Attitude. We know that everything we possess must ultimately be left behind. We also know that some will accumulate more than others. Why, then, do so many people struggle to accumulate possessions to the exclusion of nearly everything else?

_____

Is God interested in our ability to accumulate material possessions? Why or why not?

_____

3. Read and evaluate the following verses in light of seeking a proper attitude.
   a. 2 Peter 3:11

   _____

   b. Matthew 6:19-20

   _____

   c. Proverbs 11:28

   _____

The Christian's Wealth

Above all else, God is concerned with our *attitude*. The abundance or the lack of money does not affect our relationship to Him—only our attitude does.

The Christian must be able to trust God in *every* circumstance, believing that He loves us and gives us only the stewardship we can handle without being tempted beyond that which we can withstand. Because of its tangibility, money is a testing ground before God of our *true* willingness to surrender self to Him.

Wealth is neither *moral nor immoral*. There is no inherent virtue in poverty—there are dishonest poor as well as rich. God condemns the misuse of or preoccupation with wealth—not the wealth itself. The production of wealth is implied in Romans 12:5, 8 where the gift of giving is listed as a spiritual gift.

How can Christians recognize the proper attitude toward wealth when so much "folklore" surrounds this area? By understanding and accepting God's attitudes.

1. What does God say about money and happiness?

   a. 1 Timothy 6:17

   _____

   b. Psalm 17:15

   _____

   c. Proverbs 11:4

   _____

2. Does God condemn the wealthy?

   a. Psalm 8:6 _____

   b. Proverbs 28:12 _____

   c. Proverbs 22:4 _____

   _____

3. What attitude does God expect from us?

   a. Proverbs 3:16-17 _____

   b. Proverbs 3:19 _____

   c. Proverbs 3:4-6 _____

   d. 2 Peter 1:6_____

   _____

4. What can we expect from Him?

   a. Proverbs 8:18 _____

   b. Proverbs 9:11 _____

   _____

5. How does God define the *real* danger of money?

   a. 1 Timothy 6:10 _____

   b. Matthew 19:23 _____

   _____

2

God's Will in Finances

God's Will in Finances

Stewardship

The key to understanding God's will in finances is the proper understanding of *stewardship.* By Webster's definition, a steward is "one who manages another's property." We are merely stewards of God's property while we are on earth. He can choose to entrust us with as much or as little as *He* desires, but in no case will we ever take ownership.

If we Christians can accept that role as stewards and manage God's resources according to His direction, God will continue to entrust us with even more. But why would He entrust more property to one who began to hoard and who felt he was the owner? Moreover, until the Christian acknowledges God's total ownership, he can't experience God's direction in financial management.

1. Review Matthew 25:14-30 and evaluate.

   a. To what did Christ equate this parable?

   _____

   b. Why was each given a different amount?

   _____

   c. Did the owner ask all to earn the same?

   _____

   d. How were the two faithful servants rewarded?

   _____

   _____

   e. What happened to the last?

   _____

What was the keynote in this parable? Stewardship. Each using his ability, managing his master's resources well, and returning them to him.

2. Compare the parable of the steward with that found in Luke 12:16-20.

   a. How is this farmer described?

   _____

   b. Did God object to his wealth?

   _____

   c. Where did the farmer go wrong?

   _____

   d. Why did God rebuke him?

   _____

   _____

   _____

3. Read and describe the elements of becoming God's steward in Luke 12:25-34.

   a. Luke 12:25-26—How does God assess our abilities as owners?

   _____

   b. Luke 12:27, 31—What is God's promise to us?

   _____

   c. Luke 12:32—What should our attitude be?

   _____

   d. Luke 12:33—What does God ask of us?

   _____

   e. Luke 12:34—Why?

   _____

Seeing God's Wisdom in Money

God uses money in a Christian's life to direct him. If we are seeking His wisdom, He promises to supply it. But understand that God's will is not always coincidental with our wishes. God will often withhold funds in order to teach us a lesson. Too often Christians strike out on their own without clear direction from God. Not only does that violate the principle expressed in Matthew 4:7, which states, *"Jesus said to him, 'On the other hand, it is written, you shall not tempt the Lord your God,'"* but those who do it regularly have also not *truly* accepted God's wisdom as superior.

This study will help you discover the irrefutable wisdom in handling money God's way and how He uses it to instruct us.

How God Uses Finances

1. Trust:

In Matthew 6:32-33, God makes a promise to us. State that promise in your own words.

_____

_____

What is the prerequisite for its being fulfilled?

_____

19

2. Ability to Supply:

For what can we trust God if we are in His will?

Read Mark 11:24 _____

3. Trustworthiness:

God expects certain minimums from us. Read Luke 16:11. Here God equates

_____ to _____. Thus, He is verifying

our _____.

4. Love:

Many Christians fail to trust God because inwardly they believe God wants to deprive and punish them. What does Matthew 7:11 promise?

_____

This promise demonstrates God's _____ for us.

5. Power:

God wants to show us that He can do what He says.
Romans 10:11-12 promises:

a. Whoever _____ will not be disappointed.

b. God does not _____.

c. Who can participate in God's riches? _____

6. Unification:

God uses material possessions to unify the Body of Christ.
Second Corinthians 8:14 has a two-fold message.

a. When should we share? _____

b. Why? _____

Second Corinthians 8:15 describes God's plan for our surpluses.

TOO MUCH + TOO LITTLE = ENOUGH.

7. Direction:

One of the most important characteristics of a Christian's commitment is *patience*. It is virtually impossible to be obedient and impatient at the same time. God will use resources (money) as one of the tests of our obedience to His will rather than our own. Read Proverbs 3:5-6 and comment.

a. Trust _____

b. Do not trust _____

c. Then He will _____

In your own words, what is the primary message in Galatians 6:9?

_____

_____

8. Witness:

One of the most effective witnesses to many non-Christians is the use of money. It is one thing to *say* you love others, but do you *show* that love? Read Deuteronomy 15:11. What does this imply is the first requirement for helping others?

_____

Read Matthew 25:45 and compare this to the verse in Deuteronomy. Christ compares those in need to:

_____

3

The Perils of Money

"Which of you by being anxious can add a single cubit to his life's span?" (Matthew 6:27).

The Perils of Money

Servitude to Money

Just as God uses money to enhance and direct our lives, Satan will use it to shackle us. Christians should learn to recognize the danger of money entanglements and financial bondage.

What is bondage? Until recent times financial bondage meant precisely that—physical bondage. If a man could not pay his debts, he was thrown into debtor's prison, and his family then belonged to the lender. In Scripture, we see the same practice enforced against debtors:

"Make friends quickly with your opponent at law while you are with him on the way; in order that your opponent may not deliver you to the judge, and the judge to the officer, and you be thrown into prison. Truly I say to you, you shall not come out of there, until you have paid up to the last cent" (Matthew 5:25-26).

Physical bondage no longer exists, but it has been replaced by another that is equally bad—*worry* or *mental bondage*. Thousands of families each year are destroyed by financial worries caused by financial pressures (bondage). Why? Because they have violated one or more scriptural principles.

It is not simply the *lack* of money that results in bondage. Many times an *abundance* will result in mental anguish. If there is too little, people worry about gaining more, and with too much, they worry about losing it. It is always *attitude* that is reflected in God's Word. That is what *we* will examine.

25

1. Attitude:

   Read Proverbs 30:7-9. Two principles are discussed.

   a. The danger in riches is _____

   b. The danger in poverty is _____

   The principle is clear when dealing with poverty (honesty vs. dishonesty). But the distinction is not so clear with wealth. Why? We become *content* without God.

2. God's Attitude Toward Debt:

   There is much confusion regarding whether a Christian should borrow money. Our study will be directed to the biblical attitude about bondage. Let me first define *debt,* or *bondage.* Debt is when someone has delinquent financial obligations. Therefore, money borrowed and repaid according to agreement is not a *debt,* but an obligation. However, bondage can also occur if other principles are violated, as we will see later.

3. Bondage Through Debt:

   One of the most common causes of bondage is the abuse of credit. In Proverbs 22:7, God says:

   The borrower becomes _____

   This principle should tell Christians God's attitude toward delinquent debts. When someone borrows beyond his *normal* ability to repay, it is because he lacked the self-discipline to either save for the object or to deny himself a material desire.

4. Indulgence:

   God speaks to the *attitude,* not the *act.* The fact that someone is in debt is the result of an earlier attitude. Read and discuss Luke 12:15 in this regard.

   Beware of _____

   Read Proverbs 21:17. Does this mean God disallows any kind of pleasure or enjoyment? _____ Can you think of a Scripture we have used previously relating to this?

   _____

5. Avoiding Debts:

Is it scriptural to claim bankruptcy? It seems logical that if someone has incurred excessive debts and has a truly changed attitude, he should be able to start afresh, doesn't it? Read Psalm 37:21.

How is the evil man described? _____

_____

Now read Luke 16:12. Describe God's principle of credit in your own words.

_____

_____

Is God's plan logical? In worldly terms, to avoid debtors seems logical. A common response of the borrower is: "How will I live if they take everything?" Read and evaluate Psalm 50:14-15.

What does God promise? _____

What does He expect? _____

God always looks into the "heart" of a believer. As one reads in Genesis how God asked Abraham to sacrifice his son Isaac, it becomes apparent that God asked him to surrender "all." God looked into his heart and saw a true commitment to His will. Abraham believed that if God could send him a son in his old age, He could surely retrieve his son from death. Thus, God entrusted to Abraham His kingdom on earth.

When Christians transfer assets simply to avoid detachment by creditors, it reflects a basic lack of trust and deceitful attitude.

6. Bondage Through Wealth:

Financial bondage can also exist through an abundance of money. Those who use their money for self-satisfaction or hoard it for the elusive "rainy day" that never comes are also bound.

The accumulation of wealth and the physical possession of money can become an obsession that will destroy health, family, and friends. Suddenly everything and everybody becomes an object to be used in the "ladder of success."

_____

Read and evaluate Job 31:24-25.

What was Job stressing as the danger in having riches? _____

_____

What lesson can we learn about wealth and attitude? _____

_____

This attitude is not confined to non-Christians. Many Christians fall into Satan's snare and convert the very resource God provided for their peace and comfort into something full of pain and sorrow.

As noted earlier, God does not condemn wealth. He condemns the *misuse* of wealth. We will evaluate different characteristics of the perils of money. Some are brought about by too little money; some by too much. But in either case, *attitude* is the key.

Conditions of Servitude

In order to find God's financial solutions, it is first necessary to assess the problems. Too many times we treat symptoms rather than problems. As previously discussed, circumstances are merely symptoms of an earlier wrong attitude.

A Christian can assess whether a problem attitude exists if any of the following symptoms apply:

1. Overdue Bills:

   Anxiety, frustration, and worry are produced when family bills cannot be paid.

   What is the admonition in Proverbs 3:27?

   _____

   Now evaluate Proverbs 3:28. What is the Lord's direction?

   _____

   This principle establishes a pay-as-you-go system.

2. Worry About Investments:

   This may involve not only investments, but also savings and anything else that diminishes a Christian's spiritual faith.

   Review Matthew 6:24.

   God condemns _____ to money, not its possession.

   Evaluate Luke 9:25. Do you sense the same attitude in Christ's words? _____

3. "Get-Rich-Quick" Attitude:

   This attitude is not one of application as much as motivation. In other words, it is not so much *what* you do as *why* you do it.

   Is the primary motivation *work for gain* or *profit without effort*?

29

God establishes two promises in Proverbs 28:20. Explain each in your own words.

a. Faithful man _____

b. Hasty _____

_____

In Proverbs 28:22 the one who seeks quick riches is _____

What is God's assessment of him? _____

4. Laziness:

God specifically condemns this *attitude* and establishes guidelines for other Christians to follow in their relationships with Him.

Proverbs 21:25-26 describes this foolish attitude. Describe this attitude in your own words.

_____

How does God tell us to treat those who will not work (see in 2 Thessalonians 3:10)?

_____

Remember—this means those who *will not* work, not those who *cannot*.

5. Deceitfulness:

Deceitfulness refers to not only purposefully lying to others, but also not being entirely and openly honest. Our society seems to believe one cannot be both successful and honest. That is another lie promoted by Satan.

Review Proverbs 19:1.

God equates a _____ to a _____.

There are no little or "white" lies in God's evaluation. Explain Luke 16:10 in your own words.

_____

God makes a promise to those who deal deceitfully in Proverbs 20:17.

What do you think "afterward" refers to? _____

_____

6. Greediness:

An attitude of consistently desiring more than is presently owned or always wanting the best characterizes greed.

Job 21:17 describes the reward of the "wicked."

_____

What is Christ's admonition in Luke 12:15?

_____

7. Covetousness:

Desiring that which someone else has is most frequently promoted by the advertising media as "keeping up with the Joneses."

How does Psalm 73:2-3 describe this condition?

_____

Read 1 Corinthians 5:11. What is God's directive here?

_____

Does this refer to the non-Christian?_____

8. Family Needs Unmet:

Because of past debts, investments, or irresponsibility, the needs of a family may not be met. Those who give their surplus to any activity while members of their family go without basic necessities are outside of God's will.

Read Matthew 15:5-6. What did Christ say about the needs of the family?

_____

Now review 1 Timothy 5:8. How does God assess the lack of family provision?

_____

9. Overcommitment to Work:

When we reverse priorities in our lives we suffer spiritually and financially. The Bible refers to basic commitments. Describe them in your own words.

a. Matthew 6:33 _____

b. Genesis 2:24 _____

c. Psalm 127:2 _____

10. Money Entanglements:

Entanglements are the devious entrapments created by juggling the bills to keep afloat, and worldly commitments that keep many Christians out of God's service.

Read 2 Timothy 2:4. What is a typical entanglement in today's generation?

_____

Second Peter 2:20 describes what must be a "backslider." Why is the second condition worse than the first?

_____

11. Self-Indulgence:

A self-indulgent attitude is normally characterized by irresponsible spending for items that yield temporary satisfaction and little utility.

Read Luke 8:14. Does this refer to Christians? _____

List three factors that result in an unfruitful life.

a. _____

b. _____

c. _____

12. Financial Superiority:

We don't usually think of this as an example of servitude to money, but it certainly is. Scripture describes not only its characteristics, but also its dangers.

Read Ezekiel 7:19. How does God view financial worth?

_____

First Timothy 6:17 tells us God's attitude toward the rich. Describe it in your own words.

_____

_____

13. Financial Resentment:

Many people in financial difficulty blame everybody else for their problems. In actuality they have never come under God's authority and yielded to *His* wisdom. They inwardly resent God. *Attitude* again is the keynote in God's plan.

Read Proverbs 15:16. Is the reward from God always financial? _____

Answer the question asked in Romans 11:34.

The Principle About Borrowing

Before we leave this study on servitude or bondage, I would like to examine God's attitude about *credit*. This area of finances causes more chaos in Christian families than any other.

We will examine credit from the *range* of God's will. That means we must understand what responses on our part are within an acceptable range for God. Within that range God will direct us to a specific response that is His will for us. What is acceptable for me may be wrong for you. That is God's *perfect* will, and it is a very narrow channel in the *range*.

Read Psalm 37:21. How does God evaluate someone who does not repay?

_____

Read Luke 6:34-35.

v. 34—This "side of the channel" is to _____

        but without _____

v. 35—God says to expect_____

        from others.

These verses relate to the *needy* only. Thus, we discover that one end of the range in God's will is not even to be debt free (Romans 13:8), but to lend liberally from our surplus. Many Christians are debt free but are still outside of God's will by virtue of their selfishness.

4

Release from Servitude

"Long life is in her [wisdom's] right hand; in her
left hand are riches and honor. Her ways are
pleasant ways, and all her paths are peace"
(Proverbs 3:16-17).

Release from Servitude

Freedom from Worry

Just as the perils of money cause frustration and worry, God's plan provides peace and freedom. Those qualities show themselves in every aspect of a Christian's life—the release from tension and worry about overdue bills, a clear conscience, and the sure knowledge that God is in control again. That is not to say that a Christian's life will be financially trouble-free. We are human and subject to making mistakes. But once God is in charge of our finances, His divine correction will bring this area back under control.

There are steps to achieving God's plan. For every promise God makes to us, He has a prerequisite. In each case, some action is required to bring His power into focus in our lives. That might be prayer, fasting, or simply believing, but it will always require a free act of our will.

A Christian who is seeking God's best in his life must be willing to submit to His will and direction. There are many Christians who *say* they accept God's direction, but their actions deny it. They follow only when it is *convenient* to do so. Remember, God's will is not always compatible with our wishes.

Steps to Freedom

1. Transfer Ownership to God.

   Christians must realize there is no substitute for this step. If you believe *you* are the owner of even a single possession, then the ups and downs affecting that possession will be reflected in your attitude. If, however, you have made a transfer of *all* ownership to God, you will realize that the event is God's way of moving providentially to accomplish His will.

   Proverbs 3:19 defines who the *real* owner is.

   Why should we seek God's total control? Read Proverbs 8:18.

   God promises _____, _____, _____, and _____.

2. Get Out of Debt.

Let me define *debt* as I interpret it from Scripture.

A scriptural condition of debt exists when any of the following circumstances are true:

—Money, goods, or services are owed to other people with *payments past due.*
—The total of unsecured *liabilities exceeds total assets* (in other words, if a calamity took place, there would be a negative balance).
—Financial responsibilities *produce anxiety.* God will give a sense of peace when finances are managed according to His will.

a. Evaluate *every* purchase *before* buying (Proverbs 18:15).

—Does it enhance God's work through you?
—Is it a necessity?
—Can you do without it?
—Is it the best possible buy?
—Does it add to your family relationships?
—Will it depreciate quickly?
—Will it require costly upkeep?

b. Use a written budget (Proverbs 16:9). How does this verse apply to maintaining a written budget?

_____

c. Buy on a *cash-only* basis (Romans 13:8).
How does this verse apply to a cash-only policy?

_____

d. Practice saving money regularly (Proverbs 21:20).
How does this verse apply to regular saving?

_____

3. Accept God's Direction.

Worry over investments and profits will disappear when a Christian *accepts* God's direction. We must *believe* His wisdom is superior to ours and He does care about our *every* need.

Review Matthew 6:31. Define:

Anxiety— _____

Needs— _____

Reread Psalm 127:2. It says that God gives to His beloved: _____

4. Refuse Quick Decisions.

One of the premises of get-rich-quick schemes is that they require quick decisions based on incomplete information.

Read Proverbs 21:5.

Profit comes from: _____

Poverty comes from: _____

5. Excel in Your Work.

It is impossible to be slothful if excellence is the minimum acceptable standard. Too often Christians feel they should be second best or purposely fail. That is *not* God's plan.

Read 1 Peter 4:11.

How are we to perform? _____

Why? _____

Does that sound like a loser in action? _____

6. Confession—Restitution.

God tells us to put the things of the past in the past. Often that requires first making restitution to the offended party. The lessons learned and the blessings received will be worth the sacrifice. Deceitfulness and dishonesty are abominations before God, and *effort* is required to escape those habit traps.

Read Luke 19:8.

What principle had Zacchaeus found? _____

_____

Read Matthew 5:24. Discuss the concept of giving to God to make restitution. What did Christ say to do?

_____

_____

7. Contentment.

Greediness and covetousness come as a result of discontentment. To overcome those attitudes, seek contentment in a *moderate* life-style. That may be difficult at first, but there will *never* be peace in finances otherwise.

Greed is a form of lust. If it means you must give away *all* of your surplus to achieve freedom, it is worth it.

Ephesians 5:5 has some strong admonitions.

A covetous person is likened to_____

What is the inheritance described? _____

8. Provide for Family Needs.

This principle is self-evident. If the family is going without basic needs, a Christian *must* provide them. To do so may require a drastic curtailment of life-style or fulfill-ment of wants and desires. These principles will be discussed more fully in section 5, Financial Planning.

Do you feel a family in need should own things like color televisions or two cars?

_____ Why?_____

_____ Scripture ref._____

Do you feel they should let their needs be made known? _____

Why? _____ Scripture ref. _____

Should a family in debt give a tithe? _____ Why? _____

_____ Scripture ref. _____

Use James 4:3, Matthew 5:42, and Deuteronomy 14:23 as scriptural references.

9. Balanced Commitment.

Any imbalance in a life leads to frustration and eventual problems. That is particularly true of overwork. Many Christian businessmen sacrifice their families and their per-sonal relationships with Christ and rationalize it by giving both *money*.

God wants *us* first, not our money. Families need fathers, not investors. Seek the balance God requires.

Read and discuss Proverbs 23:4-5. What is its primary teaching?

_____

James 1:11 describes the futility of overcommitment. Explain why men often fail in the midst of their pursuit.

_____

10. Sacrifice Desires.

God equates a *commitment* to riches with sin. As previously stated, that does not mean He wishes us to live in poverty. But that also does not mean Christians are to be swayed by the advertising world.

God expects us to live less than extravagantly and not to be swayed by foolish sensualism promoted by the mass media.

What is the result of indulgence according to Ecclesiastes 2:10-11?

_____

Now read Ecclesiastes 2:26. What does God supply to those who seek His way?

_____

11. Put Others First.

There is no faster way to remove feelings of financial superiority than by putting others *first*. Those who are blessed with abundance must recognize that it is a *gift*. One can't feel very egotistical about receiving a gift.

Romans 12:16 relates God's attitude. Describe the four points made.

a. _____

b. _____

c. _____

d. _____

Read Philippians 2:3-5.

How are we to regard others? _____

Why? _____

12. Accept God's Provision.

God never promised equality in provision (read Deuteronomy 15:11). But He does promise our needs will be met (sometimes through the abundance of others); therefore, each Christian has a role in God's plan and must be willing to accept God's provision without resentment.

In Luke 3:14, Christ gave three instructions to those seeking God's will.

a. _____

b. _____

c. _____

In Matthew 20:15-16, Christ describes the "danger" in resentment.

a. Describe God's right. _____

b. Describe envy (resentfulness). _____

c. What is the result? _____

_____

5

Financial Planning— God's Way (Part 1)

"The plans of the heart belong to man, but the answer . . . is from the LORD" (Proverbs 16:1).

Financial Planning—God's Way
(Part 1)

What Is Planning?

Often Christians question whether they should do *any* planning. The question is often asked, "Shouldn't a Christian depend totally on God?" Yes. But does that mean they are to sit at home and wait for God to deliver manna again? Although some *seem* to think so, that is *not* God's attitude.

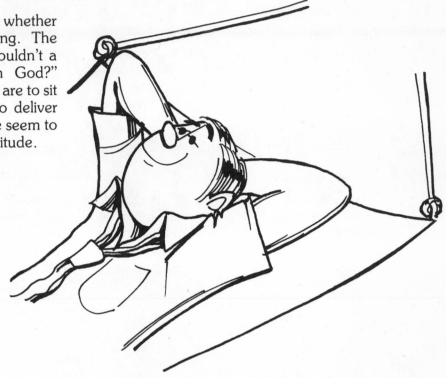

Planning is an essential element in any financial program, but particularly so for Christians. God is an orderly provider and expects the same attitude from us.

1. Discuss Proverbs 24:3-4.

    The first step in planning is to develop a *changed attitude*. That requires more than an initial try at creating plans. You must use them in *everyday* decisions.

    Don't try to develop plans with no flexibility. Remember that God's wisdom may be exercised by redirecting our paths.

2. Discuss James 1:2-3.

    Practice patience and caution in *every* financial venture. Attitude may determine the *difference between profit and loss*. Avoid any get-rich-quick schemes no matter how tempting they may seem. Stick to your plans and make no provision for hasty speculation (Proverbs 21:29).

47

Many important attitudes are necessary to develop a sound financial plan. We will review some of them in this unit. The basic areas to be discussed are:
  a. Developing short-range plans
  b. Developing long-range plans

What are short-range plans? Short-range plans are those that occur daily. Those may include paying bills, buying groceries, saving for vacation, saving for emergencies, or even paying taxes.

Everyone needs to establish short-range plans. Failure to do so will not remove their necessity, it will simply result in greater expense and anxiety.

Where to start? That is a common question. I believe the home is the first area to generate plans.

According to Proverbs 20:5 one element is necessary: _____

The Christian home should be characterized by orderliness and excellence. Neither is possible without good planning. The following principles will help you to establish useful and biblical plans. As you complete these exercises, think of how you can apply the principles in your home. In many instances the discussion questions will not have one "correct" answer but are designed to bring out individual insights in a group discussion.

Steps to Short-Range Plans

1. Establish *written* plans and goals.

   A written goal provides a visible objective standard toward which to work. In the home that plan is called a budget. (In a later unit we'll design a budget for the home.)

   Proverbs 16:3 defines how to make our plans compatible with God's will.

   What is the first step?_____

   Proverbs 16:9 describes *how* that is to be accomplished.

   What is our role? _____

   What is God's input?_____

2. Commit God's Portion First.

   Although this principle is developed more fully in the unit on sharing, it is an *essential* element in any financial plan.

   Discuss *why* that is true from the following Scripture:

   Proverbs 3:9-10 _____

   2 Corinthians 9:11 _____

3. Reduce or Eliminate the Use of Credit.

   In some families the total elimination of credit buying may not be feasible. But *every* family can reduce its use. As previously discussed, families in bondage *must* stop the use of credit to *ever* escape.

   Proverbs 27:12 describes one who proceeds in the face of future trouble as:

4. Seek God's Plan for Living Within the Budget.

Many families in financial difficulty think that generating extra income, such as the wife's working, will help. That is usually *not* the case. Generally the problems are caused by overspending, not insufficient income. More income will sometimes make the situation *worse*. If the total level of spending increases, credit will too. Families should put God's plan into action *first*.

a. *Extra Income.* Consider the possibility of additional work *only* after correcting buying habits. Working mothers sometimes contribute little income but sacrifice much in family guidance.

b. *Before purchasing, give God an opportunity to provide the item.* If our purchase is in God's will, He will sometimes manifest Himself in our finances by providing it from a totally unexpected source. One of the great joys in a Christian's life is to experience God's love through His miraculous provision.

Read 2 Chronicles 16:9—For whom does God search over the whole world?

_____

Why?_____

What practice does Psalm 37:7 teach?_____

_____ and _____

c. *Pray about every expenditure.* That experience brings God directly into our lives and strengthens our faith so that we can trust Him in greater things.

—No purchase is too large or too small to *pray* about.

—Bring your family in on the petition before God and allow them to share in the spiritual blessing.

—Learn to discern God's will in the area of new purchases. God may not grant you *every wish*, because often we ask for things that will ultimately hurt us.

—Consider two prospective purchases—pray about them before buying.

1. _____

2. _____

5. Set Your Own Goals.

Those who allow others to establish their plans and goals are going to be unhappy. Unfortunately, that is often the case. Someone is made to feel guilty because of his less worldly or aesthetic goals and allows others to change his course.

Quite often a Christian will get involved in investments or get-rich-quick schemes because others around him seem more successful.

Remember, *God* has a plan for your life. Your neighbor does not.

Read Psalm 17:15.

Discuss what contentment is and is not: _____

Proverbs 3:13-14 describes success as: _____

Proverbs 3:19 defines its source as: _____

6. Seek Good Christian Counsel.

To get help you must be willing to *ask* for it. Many Christians are willing to help others but will never ask for help themselves. *That is ego.* No one is without difficulties, and therefore each of us needs some counsel and advice.

Many Christians refuse to seek good counsel because they feel that it somehow reflects on their commitment. *That is nonsense.*

Read Proverbs 19:20. We are admonished: _____

Why? _____

Whose counsel should we seek?

a. Proverbs 23:22 _____

b. Ephesians 5:23 _____

c. Ephesians 5:31 _____

d. Proverbs 11:14 _____

Describe and discuss:

a. The qualities of a good counselor (Titus 1:6-9).

_____

_____

b. The role of a good counselor (1 Peter 5:2-3).

_____

_____

c. The result of a good counselor (2 Peter 1:6-7).

_____

_____

Weigh those characteristics against any counsel you give or receive.

6

Financial Planning— God's Way (Part 2)

Financial Planning—God's Way
(Part 2)

Establishing Long-Range Plans

What are long-range goals? These are the result of short-range plans linked back-to-back. Few Christians make any organized short-range plans; even fewer make any long-range plans. For example, if allowed to progress by normal standards, our level of living will expand to compete with that of any nonbeliever. Faced with a large money surplus, the normal tendency is to "store" it for future protection. Without any pre-arranged plan we buy excessive insurance, store useless assets, and determine to either impoverish our children or hopelessly spoil them after we are gone.

Long-range planning God's way will *provide* but not *protect*. It will insure your resource is an *asset*, not a *liability*.

Steps to Establishing Long-Range Plans

1. As with short-range planning, a written plan is always best.

   In the last section of this study you will find forms to help you plan.

   Why is planning and follow-up necessary (Proverbs 27:23-24)?

   _____

2. Establish maximum financial goals rather than minimum.

   Normally we fix our goals on attaining riches and establish some motives for accumulating money. At first the amount may be a few thousand dollars, but it is quickly adjusted as the funds are available.

   God's plan is that we establish a maximum goal and predetermine not to allow excessive accumulation.

55

Read and evaluate 1 Timothy 6:18-19.
God instructs us to:

a. _____

b. _____

c. _____

Storing what? _____

What is our promised reward? _____

Read Luke 8:18.

Does this verse mean "the rich get richer and the poor get poorer," as we commonly hear? _____

How does this relate to the same admonition in Luke 19:26? _____

_____

3. Establish a Long-Range Family Plan.

Family goals are fundamental to future success. If they are made according to God's principles, the rewards will pass from parents to children. But, unless you have sound family plans and goals, how can you expect your children to become financially responsible?

a. *A family sharing plan.* It is vitally important that the whole family be made a part of God's sharing plan. Husbands and wives should discuss this with their children. Give your children the joy of sharing from their resources also. These attitudes learned early will pay dividends in freedom from financial obsessions and greed. Paul said in 1 Corinthians 3:13 that each man's work will become evident.

How does this relate to teaching your children about freely sharing?

_____

Read Proverbs 13:22.

What is the inheritance referred to here? _____

_____

b. *A family living plan.* If you never establish any standard of living for your family, others will. Families need to know the boundaries within which they can operate, and failure to establish those will result in overspending and ultimate bondage.

1 Peter 3:3-4 relates to a *reasonable* standard of living. What is it?

_____

_____

Does that Scripture rule out any adornment?_____

What is the required balance? _____

Read 1 Peter 3:7.

Husbands are to_____their wives.

They are to recognize and appreciate her _____.

Wives are to be treated as _____ heirs.

Every family must recognize the difference between needs, wants, and desires in life.

In Matthew 6:32 God recognizes our _____ and promises to supply.

Identify the basic levels of expenditures:

Needs — 1 Timothy 6:8 describes them as: _____

_____

Wants — Luke 3:11 describes wants as: _____

_____

Desires — (lavishness) 1 John 2:15-16 describes them as:_____

_____

Those differences can be illustrated by various products and their uses. For example, we all need clothing. That *need* can be satisfied by simple, basic garments. (Such as chain store apparel.)

Wants may be met by buying in an elite shop for fashion designs.

Desires may be satisfied by imported or exclusive clothing to dazzle other people.

Every basic purchase in the home should be assessed by its category and allowed or disallowed according to God's plan for *your* family.

c. *A family savings plan.* Many families fail to save any money and consequently are always borrowing to buy. Even a minor financial setback plunges them into panic and anxiety.

Read Proverbs 21:20.

The wise man _____.

The foolish man _____.

Later we will evaluate the difference between saving (provision) and hoarding (protection).

d. *A family inheritance plan.* Consider the consequences of large amounts of money left your family either outright or in trust. Do you believe God will provide, or that He dies with you? Remember, God demands that we *provide* for our families, not *protect* them. Later we will discuss how much you can or should leave, but always evaluate it in light of *God's* plan, not the world's.

Read Luke 9:59-62. This man wanted his father's inheritance, which could only be received after the official burial.

Was his father's inheritance a blessing or a curse? _____

What is God's promise for descendants in Psalm 37:25? _____

_____

4. Establish a Long-Range Earning Plan.

As we noted in short-range planning, many people allow others to set their financial goals. Often losses are suffered because someone is talked into a new method of seeking riches. Whether or not it is a get-rich-quick scheme or a legitimate investment program, doesn't matter. If it is not in line with your personal goals for earning money, you will suffer.

Read Psalm 49:16-17.

God says not to _____ anyone.

What is the reward for accumulating only money?_____

In Hebrews 13:5 God says:

Stay away from _____

and _____

5. Establish a Contingency (or Surplus) Plan.

Once a maximum standard of living is established most Christians can expect to accumulate a surplus. You must predetermine the application of that surplus or it will be consumed through life-style adjustments and hoarding.

With the best of intentions, many Christians keep the Lord's surplus. Decide on a positive contingency plan in the event God supplies an abundance. Why should He choose you to receive His riches?

Review again Luke 3:11.

What is Christ's contingency plan for our surplus? _____

_____

6. Establish Every Long-Range Plan in Light of God's Principles.

   a. *Honesty.* God will accept nothing less than complete honesty. Every plan must take that into consideration.

   The most common violation of honesty, I believe, is tax evasion. Christians who are otherwise honest cheat on their taxes and rationalize that they feel the laws are unfair. To take every tax avoidance is both logical and legal, but to evade taxes is illegal and dishonest. The lines are very narrow, and Christians must constantly be aware of the subtleties Satan will lay before us, all in the guise of shrewd "opportunities."

   Read Romans 13:6-7.
   God says that government leaders are _____

   Verse 7 says "tax to whom it is due." That is the same admonition given to the repayment of *debts* in Proverbs.

   Matthew 17:24-27 relates that even Christ paid taxes, though He was legally exempt.
   Why did He do so? (v. 27) _____
   What principle does that show for us?_____

   _____

   b. *Welfare of employees.* Christian employers and supervisors should be aware that authority is not a *right*—it is a *responsibility.* God establishes the principle that He will defend workers when they are wronged without cause. A Christian employer's long-range plans should include the welfare and advancement of his workers' interest as well as his own.

   Deuteronomy 24:14 relates the principle of not oppressing workers. Does this apply only to believers? _____

   _____

   Why do you think that is?_____

   _____

Once a Christian employer adopts God's principle of becoming a witness in every aspect of his business, a revolution will occur, both in employee attitude and company productivity.

Employers should be aware of their responsibilities to treat employees fairly and pay a *fair* wage.

If you are an employer, I challenge you to establish at least two long-range plans for the enhancement of your employees' welfare.

1— _____

_____

2— _____

_____

c. *Employee responsibility.* Just as employers must stand responsible for their workers' welfare, employees have a responsibility to their vocational authority. As we studied earlier, *excellence* is the minimum standard acceptable to God. Also *honor* is the minimum attitude presentable to an employer. If all employees did everything possible to enhance the lives of their employers, friction and resentments would be eliminated.

Read Colossians 3:23—24.
In these Scriptures we find several principles.

1—Work for _____ rather than _____

2—The employer is held in the same authority relationship as Christ. Explain why. _____

_____

3—What is the worker's promised reward? _____

_____

Examine your own work situation and decide what *you* can do to improve your work and help your supervisor succeed.

1— _____

2— _____

3— _____

7

Motives for Accumulating Wealth

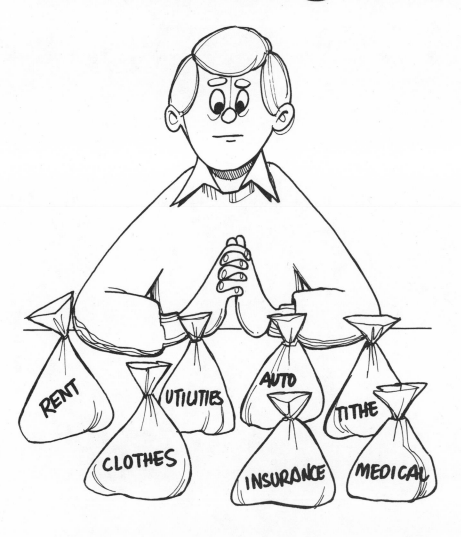

"Let a man meet a bear robbed of her cubs, rather than a fool in his folly" (Proverbs 17:12).

Motives for Accumulating Wealth

God's Attitude

We have reviewed what wealth is in God's terms. Now we will examine *why* one should accumulate wealth. Accumulation here means more than "storing away." Accumulation refers to making, using, and spending money.

Money can yield comfort and convenience, and it can provide the means for spreading the gospel of Jesus Christ.

But money can also become the object of devotion and idolatry. Love of money can separate families, spoil children, and breed dishonesty.

Therefore, it is vitally important to understand why God would have us as Christians accumulate wealth.

God has provided a ministry in money for many Christians—a ministry of giving. Once Christians accept giving as a ministry, a whole new area of God's Word becomes clear.

> "And God is able to make all grace abound to you, that always having all sufficiency in everything, you may have an abundance for *every* good deed" (2 Corinthians 9:8).

If you have the ability to make money, you *must* have the ability to share money.

> "Instruct them to do good, to be rich in good works, to be generous and ready to share" (1 Timothy 6:18).

Many people think that to give is gracious but to gain is wrong. Clearly, in order to give money one must be able to make money. Accept that principle and ingrain it in your personality—making money can be a part of your ministry. You may have other ministries as well, but many committed Christians are gifted in the ministry of making and giving money to the Lord's work.

> "But just as you abound in everything, in faith and utterance and knowledge and in all earnestness and in the love we inspired in you, see that you abound in this gracious work also. I am not speaking this as a command, but as proving through the earnestness of others the sincerity of your love also" (2 Corinthians 8:7-8).

In this Unit we will discuss various motives for making and storing money both from the world's perspective and from God's. Before going any further list some of the reasons you think people do so and how those motives fit into a Christian's financial plans.

1— _____

2— _____

3— _____

4— _____

5— _____

Here we will look at motives and methods for accumulation. In section 2 we discussed the *range* of God's will in terms of the channel. In this section we will observe accumulation from that same perspective so that you can decide whether or not your plans are within God's will.

Why People Accumulate Money

1. Because Others Advise Them To.

   Just as many people allow others to set their goals, they also allow a friend or acquaintance to talk them into financial schemes. They will commit time and money to efforts they know little or nothing about and neglect more important functions.

   Should we let others advise us on how to make money?

   Read Proverbs 15:22.

   a. God advises we: _____

   _____

   b. Why? _____

   _____

   Now read Proverbs 14:15.

   a. A simple man (simpleton) is described as: _____

   _____

   b. A prudent man (wise): _____

   _____

   Do you see the range (channel) of God's will?

Proverbs 15:22   Proverbs 14:15
(Seek counsel)   (Weigh all advice)

2. Many People Seek Wealth Because They Envy Others.

   As we discussed in section 2, this is sometimes called covetousness or greed. Today we label it "social pressure." How does God view this motive?

   _____

Read Psalm 73:2-3.

Slipping from God's path is caused by what? _____

_____

Read Luke 12:15.

God warns us to beware of _____

Why? _____

Have you *ever* kept a good relationship with someone you envied or who envied
what you had? _____

Why? _____

Have you purposely tried to make others envious of you? _____

Why? _____

Can you see the range of God's will?_____

There isn't any. God *does not* allow this motive for Christians.

3. The Game of Making Money.

   Have you ever known someone who was pursuing (or being pursued by) the money
   game? Everybody becomes a pawn—family, friends, fellow Christians.

   It is unfortunate that we help promote this attitude by elevating the "winners." The
   game of money will soon overwhelm the players until it is a "no holds barred" con-
   test.

   One of the characteristics of this motive is the inability to accept a loss.

   Proverbs 17:12 describes this type of individual as a _____

   _____

   What is the range of God's will? _____

   Why? _____

4. Accumulation for Self-Esteem.

This motive is a particularly disastrous one because most of us feed this weakness. Those who accumulate for self-esteem do so that others may feed their egos.

These are the social butterflies who attend only the "important" events and associate only with the "right" people. They purchase esteem from everyone, including their families. They never give unless it is recognized and never share except to promote themselves.

Read 1 Timothy 6:17.

a. This gives direction in how to address whom? _____

b. How are they admonished? _____

_____

c. What is the advice given? _____

_____

Read Proverbs 16:18.

a. Pride leads to _____

b. A haughty spirit leads to _____

What is the range? _____

Money is neither good nor bad, moral nor immoral. It is the use of it, the pattern of your life, and your perspective that counts.

5. Accumulation for the Love of Money.

Those who accumulate because they love money would not part with it even for esteem. Their lives are usually characterized by hoarding and abasement. They possess thousands or millions of dollars, but the loss of even a small portion is traumatic.

Have you ever known anyone who was in love with his money? Could his life be summarized as one of greed and bitterness? _____

69

Read 1 Timothy 6:10.

a. What is the root of many evils? _____

Ecclesiastes 5:10 contains two principles. What are they?

a. _____

b. _____

What word does verse 10 use to describe those attitudes? _____

Assess God's will. _____

_____

6. Accumulation for "Protection."

Many people feel they must accumulate wealth for *protection*. Apparently they don't believe God can supply their needs, so they accumulate hoards of wealth. At first the goal is a few thousand, just to protect against future uncertainties. But allowed to expand, the amount is inconsequential; there will *never* be *enough* protection. Again, there is nothing wrong with planning and saving God's way. But anyone who hoards for protection does not believe God is true to His Word. In our society protection is promoted as all important. We are bombarded by the "need" for enormous amounts of life insurance, health insurance, disability, liability, etc. How many of those plans reflect any aspect of God's Word?

Read Psalm 50:14-15.

a. God says in our day of trouble _____

_____

b. His promise is_____

_____

Read Ecclesiastes 5:13.
What is the evil described?_____

_____

The obsession over protection takes away something that God would have us live by, the very reason we are saved—*faith and trust in God.*

What is God's will?_____

70

7. Accumulating to Supply a Spiritual Gift.

There is *only one* reason God allows us a surplus—to enable us to *give*. True wealth comes from the gift of giving. God promises His blessings on all who share freely. Paul explains this reason for having wealth in Romans 12. The gift of giving provides the foundation for a life of selfless devotion to others who are deserving.

> "You will be enriched in everything for all liberality, which through us is producing thanksgiving to God" (2 Corinthians 9:11).

Being rich or poor is a matter of providence for the Christian. But the responsibility of being a wealthy Christian is greater than that of being a poor Christian. Because of the temptations, God often speaks of the dangers of assuming a worldly attitude about money.

Read 2 Corinthians 9:6.

a. The first promise is: _____

_____

b. The second is: _____

_____

Thus, the range of God's will can be found in a single verse.

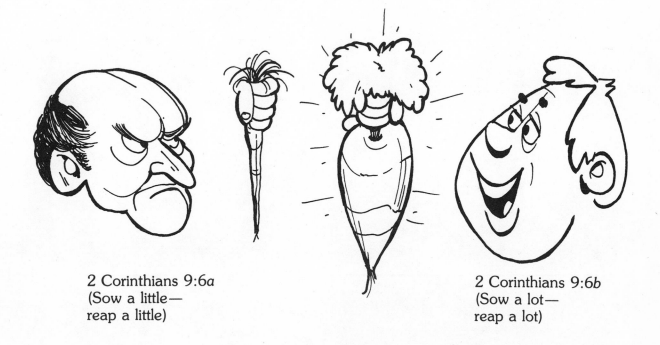

2 Corinthians 9:6a
(Sow a little—
reap a little)

2 Corinthians 9:6b
(Sow a lot—
reap a lot)

8

How Much Is Enough?

"Better is a little with the fear of the LORD, than great treasure and turmoil with it" (Proverbs 15:16).

How Much Is Enough?

Living Expenses, Investments, Retirement, and Inheritance

Now that we have evaluated the various motives for accumulating money, we will examine the question of how much is enough. Each of us is involved with making, spending, saving, and sharing the wealth God supplies. But how much should logically fit into each category?

MAKING SPENDING SAVING SHARING

1. How Much Current Provision?

Current provision is the composite of living standard and short-term cash reserves. It is not "protection" for the family, nor is it the *exact* standard for everyone. No two families will have the same goals within God's will or the same standard of living. His range is usually wide enough to allow for many individual differences. But it does have specific limits and those set our life-styles.

Those who make no provision for their families are clearly outside of God's plan and suffer as a result. Those who hoard and live lavishly are also outside of God's plan and suffer accordingly.

Read Proverbs 24:30-34.

a. What is the chief characteristic described in verses 30 and 31?

_____

_____

b. What is the result of that characteristic? _____

_____

Now read Proverbs 12:11.

Prosperity comes from what? _____

As expressed in Proverbs 18:11, riches are: _____

_____

75

Luke 6:24-25.

a. How does Christ describe those who indulge themselves?

_____

b. What is their ultimate reward? _____

_____

These verses help a Christian construct a life-style according to God's plan:

a. Slothfulness is not tolerated—Proverbs 24:30.
b. Overwork is not acceptable—Psalm 127:2.
c. God encourages some saving—Proverbs 21:20.
d. God abhors one who hoards—Ephesians 5:5.
e. Family "protection" is not possible—Psalm 50:14-15.
f. Family provision is God's minimum and maximum—Hebrews 13:5.

2. How Much for Investments?

Naturally, if a part of your ministry is the ability to make money and give it, you need an investment reserve. You should retain funds out of each investment to make additional investments. Too many people believe that amount is 100 percent. They take 100 percent of the proceeds of the first investment and put it into a new investment. Sometimes that is done for tax advantages to defer income, but it is not scriptural. God is capable of using His money in His ministry *today*. Many investors will be disappointed when, after having kept the Lord's money for years and never grasping the opportunity to share in His work, they realize it's gone.

Remember the parable of the servants in Luke 19:11-26? Several principles were presented.

a. God *selects* some to be investors.
b. He expects them to use their "talents" well.
c. He expects the return of *most* or all of the proceeds.

This parable establishes the lowest end of God's will for investors. They must be chosen by Him (we will later examine how to find God's plan) and must be willing to reinvest in His work.

Now read Acts 4:32-35.

a. How is stewardship described? _____

b. What was the motive behind the act? _____

3. How Much for Retirement?

How much is enough for retirement? Many people think they need to be able to spend a hundred times as much money at retirement as they spent during the rest of their lives. That's not true. Once you set a pattern for living during your life, it won't change after retirement except to decrease in some instances. Even that is not a great change in most cases because your standard of living has leveled off. Christians who accumulate hoards of dollars, ultimately to be used for retirement, are fooling themselves.

Retirement, as we know it, is a relatively new innovation. Two or three generations ago few people believed it was necessary to stop all activity simply because one was 62 or 65 years old. That same philosophy will again be evident when most of the modern day programs prove to be insolvent. That does not mean that you cannot plan toward a less productive period of advanced age, but it does mean that your plans should be compatible with God's purpose for you at 65 and above.

God speaks about fulfillment throughout a lifetime in Ecclesiastes 5:19-20.

a. When God supplies wealth it is for: _____

_____

b. When someone works according to God's plan, his gift is: _____

_____

c. How is his age described? _____

_____

Read Luke 12:30-31.
God's promise is: _____

_____

What is His prerequisite? _____

_____

What is God's promise in Psalm 37:28? _____

_____

Thus, God will allow some accumulation in prospect of advancing years, but He will not allow hoarding. That transfers dependence from God to money.

Anyone who believes they can store "enough" for the future had better reassess where we are and what the future holds. Are you willing to trust God totally and accept His Word as true?

4. How Much for Inheritance?

The "mania" over protection in our society is abundantly reflected in this area. Christians who do not consider the consequences of large amounts of money in the hands of immature or unknowledgeable family members leave them vast sums in assets and insurance. We somehow believe that money provides "protection," and we develop great walled islands for our loved ones.

The need to provide for others extends beyond death if resource is available. But the story of the Prodigal Son (Luke 15:11-24) shows the result of providing in excess. At least that father was still alive to counsel his son. Paul expresses the joy of earning one's way in Acts 20:33-35.

Ask yourself in light of Paul's message:

a. Have you caused your children to covet your money?

b. Do you want them to earn their own way?

c. Would you rather have them be givers than takers?

Does this imply that a Christian is to leave no provision for his family? Absolutely not. It means that we are to *always* think in terms of *provision* not *protection*.

Read Ecclesiastes 6:3.
This verse describes a husband and father who was at death a burden to his family.

What was his error? _____

First Timothy 5:8 describes God's assessment of one who does this as: _____

_____

According to Proverbs 13:22:

What is the inheritance left by a good man? _____

_____

Remember the error of the man in Luke 9:59? His father's inheritance was a stumbling block.

Why? _____

Ecclesiastes 4:7-8 speaks to the vanity of storing riches without cause. That same assessment should be made for storing riches to the injury of one's family.

Thus, the range of God's will may well be expressed as a single reference point.

9

Sharing By God's Plan

LET **GOD** HAVE THE TIP OF THE ICEBERG!

10%

90%

"Honor the LORD from your wealth, and from the first of all your produce; so your barns will be filled with plenty, and your vats will overflow with new wine" (Proverbs 3:9-10).

Sharing by God's Plan

The Tithe—Is It Applicable?

This section speaks directly to the scriptural principles of sharing through the channels God has provided.

It is essential to understand how important God considers sharing. But first let me say that I accept the *entire* Bible as inspired by God and consider the lessons given in the Old Testament to be as important as those in the New Testament.

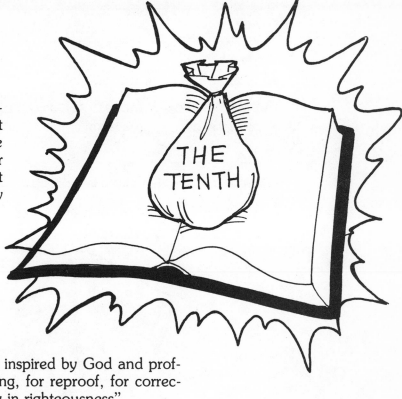

"All Scripture is inspired by God and profitable for teaching, for reproof, for correction, for training in righteousness" (2 Timothy 3:16).

In many instances Christ clarified God's principles and simplified them for us, whereas others from the Old Testament were relinquished for a higher authority. For instance, it is no longer necessary to make blood sacrifices because Christ's blood was given as the ultimate sacrifice. And no longer are we slaves to the law because Christ's death has pardoned us. But, for the Christian seeking God's will, God's principles point the way to peace, happiness, and prosperity because the author of the universe promises to manage our finances.

There are scores of Scriptures relating to the reasons for sharing from what God supplies us. Let's examine *why* God says to share.

1. The Tithe.

The tithe is often misunderstood. Some Christians believe the tithe is a legalism affecting only Old Testament Jews and has no real meaning today. Others believe tithing is a qualification for being a Christian and failure to do so will result in God's expelling us. Absolutely *neither* is correct. We will review the tithe from its origin in the Old Testament to its purpose in the New Testament.

Read Genesis 14:18-20.

a. Abram delivered an offering to Melchizedek. Why? _____

_____

Read Hebrews 7:1-10.

b. Melchizedek met Abraham (v. 1) and _____ him.

c. Who was Melchizedek (v. 2)? _____

_____

Did Abraham have the written law of Moses to obey? _____

Why did he tithe? _____

84

2. What Does the New Testament Say?

Read Matthew 23:23.

Christ reaffirmed their need to tithe although He rebuked their failure to observe the other aspects of God's law. What did He ask of them?

_____

Read 2 Corinthians 9:6.

The principle is: He who _____

will _____

Does that mean that a Christian can tithe to God with a profit motive?

_____

Read Romans 11:35 and answer.

_____

The principle is: The first part and the last part belong to *God*. He returns and multiplies to those who give *freely* and without thought for profiting. God is under no requirement to multiply our gifts. He does so because He *loves* us.

85

Turning to the Old Testament law, read Malachi 3:8.

God equates withholding of the tithe to: _____

_____

Read Malachi 3:10.

God says bring the _____

into His storehouse.

Why? _____

Read Malachi 3:11.

God promises: _____

In Deuteronomy 14:22-23:

God says to (v. 22): _____

Why did He require a tithe (v. 23b)? _____

_____

Proverbs 1:7 says fear of the Lord is what? _____

_____

Thus we give in fear (reverence) of the Lord to establish His wisdom (ownership) over our money. He then promises to watch over *all* of our wealth. Thus tithing establishes our testimony of God's *ownership*.

Sharing from Obedience

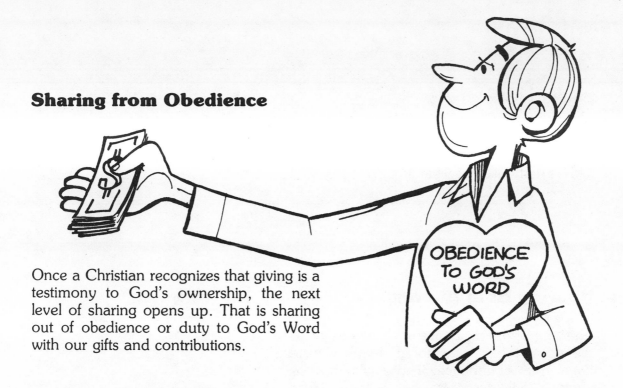

Once a Christian recognizes that giving is a testimony to God's ownership, the next level of sharing opens up. That is sharing out of obedience or duty to God's Word with our gifts and contributions.

Opportunities arise as God reveals others around us who are in need, and we recognize a responsibility to them. Those needs may be physical needs of families or material needs of Christian organizations.

1. Read Matthew 25:33-40.

   a. What is God's promise for those who obey by sharing (v. 34)? _____

   _____

   b. What does He ask us to do (vv. 35-36)? _____

   _____

   c. To what does God equate our sharing (v. 40)? _____

   _____

   According to James 2:15 we are admonished to share with those in need of:

   _____ and _____

2. Read 1 John 3:18-19.

   According to verse 18, we are to show our love in _____

   and _____

   This demonstrates what (v. 19)? _____

   _____

Sharing from Abundance

To share from abundance requires love because the norm today is to hoard. Many Christians have great abundance. Those who have surpluses should recognize that as God's blessing and seek His will for that surplus. The key to finding God's will is *love* for God and His people.

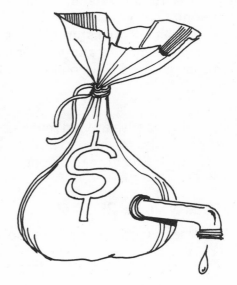

To share from abundance out of love means: I have much, and I want to share with someone who needs much. Once you give, you will find that you can't outgive God. If you continue to give, even when it seems impossible, God will show you how much He can give in return. Giving from love is one of the greatest blessings that we can have.

How does this differ from sharing out of obedience? I believe it is the next spiritual step up. We know that Christ recognizes dangers in riches and states that the rich will always have great difficulty adhering to God's plan (Matthew 19:23-24). Therefore, sharing out of abundance is practiced by the committed few who recognize God's bounty.

Read 2 Corinthians 8:15.

What is the plan in God's balance sheet?

_____ + _____ = ENOUGH.

This plan is important, and its logic is described in 2 Corinthians 8:12-14.

Giving according to (v. 12) _____

Are we to give to the wants and desires of others (v. 13)? _____

Why? _____

What can we rely on? _____

_____

Sacrificial Giving

This means of giving is available to those Christians absolutely committed to God's plan. Sacrificial giving is almost unknown to us, particularly in America. Worldly motives have clouded our thinking and dulled our sensitivity. Often our level of commitment to our brothers in need is to provide them with a ride to the welfare office. God will not allow His work to tarry for lack of funds. He will simply redistribute the necessary funds to Christians who are sincerely seeking His will and who will sacrifice personal luxuries for the need of others.

89

1. Read Luke 21:1-4.

   a. How would you describe the amount given (v. 2)? _____

   _____

   b. How did Christ assess the gift (v. 3)? _____

   _____

   c. Why? _____

   _____

2. Read Hebrews 13:16.

   a. We are admonished: _____

   b. Why? _____

3. Read 2 Corinthians 8:7-9.

   a. According to verse 7, in what are we to abound? _____

   _____

   b. As proof of what (v. 8)?_____

   _____

   c. According to verse 9, that sacrifice is equated to: _____

   _____

From God's Word, sacrifice is assessed according to *attitude,* not *amount.* Those who never forego any of their own desires or wants for the needs of others have missed a vital part of God's financial plan.

God's plan for sharing begins with:

Tithe—A testimony to God's ownership

Obedience—Helping the obvious needs around us

Abundance—Giving from our surpluses

Sacrifice—Yielding our wants and needs for others

10

Who Deserves Help?

"Even when we were with you, we used to give you this order: if anyone will not work, neither let him eat" (2 Thessalonians 3:10).

Who Deserves Help?

Don't Help Everyone—Giving to the Family

This is a popular question. Who really warrants our help? God's Word is not ambiguous.

1. Those We Are Not to Help.

   Are you surprised that God specifically directs us *not* to help someone? There are people God is correcting through material difficulties. That may be to bring them to Him or to strengthen them. For us to interfere is to presume His will. Other people are asking for wants or desires rather than needs. We can choose to help, but we are not required to.

   Read 2 Thessalonians 3:10-11 and state it in your own words.

   _____

   _____

   How are we to respond to such a situation?

   Read 2 Thessalonians 3:14-15.

   _____

   _____

Where should we help, according to Proverbs 22:9?
What is required? _____

_____

Read Proverbs 28:22.
Who is deserving? _____

_____

Luke 12:33 says:
Give to _____

According to 2 Corinthians 8:13, we are not to give for the _____
of others.

2. Sharing With Your Family.

What is a family? How are we to
help family members?

BRING HOME THE BACON!

A family, in God's Word, is more than just husband, wife, and children. It also refers to other relatives within your family such as mother, father, aunts, uncles. All are deserving of our help, provided they are unable to meet their own needs.

Read 1 Timothy 5:8.

a. A Christian *must:* _____

b. Or he has: _____

c. And is equated to an: _____

Read 1 Timothy 5:16.

We are to support our _____

(I believe this refers to the disabled also.)

Read Matthew 15:5-6.

a. Christ confronted the Pharisees because they encouraged giving gifts to the church while parents were suffering. Why is this contrary to God's law?

_____

b. Christ said they had substituted a _____
for God's Word.

Although God does not wish us to lavishly provide for our families, He will not allow an attitude of indifference. The responsibility for family members who cannot provide for themselves rests with *each* Christian—not with the government.

Sharing with the "Body"

It seems almost inconceivable that there are hungry Christians in our country today, but there are. The worst witness is to ignore the needs in the Body of Christ.

1. God's attitude is clearly stated in 1 John 3:17-18 as discussed earlier.

   If we have a *surplus* and behold a brother _____

   and fail to help, what is the conclusion? _____

   _____

   Let us not love only with _____

   but with _____

   _____

2. James stated that same attitude in James 2:15-16.

   The description is of Christians in: _____

   The command is to: _____

   _____

3. Christ Himself left us explicit directions on the same requirement. Read Matthew 24:45-46.

Christ describes one who supplies needs at the proper time as: _____

_____

One who does so is (v. 46): _____

_____

Sharing with the Shepherds

Many Christians somehow feel that the shepherds of our faith should live on a lower standard than anyone else. That is against God's Word. Spirituality is *not* proportional to poverty.

First Corinthians 9:9-11 states several principles.

A Christian soldier has a need for his living.

God commands those who hear the Word to support those who deliver it.

Describe this principle in your own words (v. 11). _____

_____

_____

1. Read 3 John 5-6.

   How are we to support ministering brethren?

   _____

   _____

2. Read 1 Corinthians 9:14.

   Describe the Lord's directive: _____

   _____

Sharing with the Unsaved:

Why would God expect us to use His money to feed the unsaved? Many Christians question whether we are to give to their needs. God's answer shows how important this is to Him by the sheer quantity of references to doing so.

It seems obvious that most Christians would recognize the need to help the Body (although even those go unmet many times). But allowed to rationalize with our own logic, we would probably exclude the unsaved. Therefore God leaves no possible misunderstanding. We are to witness by our *actions* as well as our words.

Matthew 5:42 requires:

_____ to those who ask (in need).

The *amount* is not important, only the *attitude*.

Matthew 10:42 promises a reward to:

Those who give even _____

What is the promise? _____

_____

100

Where Your Gifts Should Go

Be sensitive to God's direction in giving.

God provides opportunities not only to give to the needs of the saints, but also to invest tithes and offerings in His work. Unfortunately, the Christian is besieged by charitable requests—some are deserving, but many are poorly managed, unfruitful, or dishonest. In seeking God's direction, ask the following questions before giving:

1. Is the organization communicating a message true to Scripture?

2. Are people responding positively?

3. Is the organization seeking and accomplishing goals?

4. Are the lives of the leadership consistent with scriptural principles?

5. Is the organization multiplying itself?

6. Is there a standard of excellence along with freedom from waste? What is the ratio of money spent on fund-raising to that used by the ministry?

7. What do other Christian organizations say about it?

No one could possibly supply the needs of everyone else. Therefore, it is important to discern God's will in sharing. He will place in each Christian's heart the needs of particular individuals and organizations. Be sensitive and available to God's direction, and He will use you in His work.

Discuss these points in your group.

In Proverbs 28:27 God makes two promises.

a. One who gives to the poor will: _____

b. One who ignores the needs around him: _____

_____

It is important that Christians acquire the proper perspective concerning with whom to share and when. We have reviewed those areas from God's Word and found:

We are required to share in *needs*—not wants or desires.

We are to share with those *unable* to provide for themselves.

We are to always supply the needs of our family.

We are to provide for the ministering brethren in a manner worthy of God.

We are to provide for the needs of fellow believers.

We are to supply the needs of the poor— saved or unsaved.

11

God's Principles of
Financial Decisions

"The LORD by wisdom founded the earth; by understanding He established the heavens" (Proverbs 3:19).

God's Principles of Financial Decisions

Financial Breathing

In this section we will consolidate some of the previous principles into a plan for financial breathing. That is, exhaling bad habits and inhaling good principles. Remember, God's plan is simple. If it were not, how would most of us ever apply it? It is the Holy Spirit that simplifies it for us when we allow Him to.

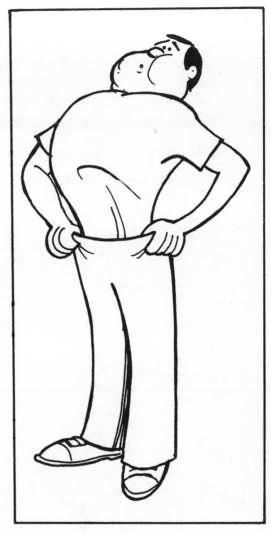

To put God's financial plan into action we must:

1. Acknowledge His Ownership—Daily.

    Be certain that daily decisions are surrendered to God. Just as problems are a daily occurrence, so is acknowledgment of God's authority.

    Proverbs 3:4-6 promises us:

    a. If we trust, we will find: _____

    b. We are not to: _____

    c. Acknowledge God and He will: _____

    _____

    What discipline is necessary to become a disciple?

    Luke 9:23 says: If anyone wants to follow Christ he must: _____

    _____

2. Accept God's Answers and Direction.

Many times we ask God for direction but we precondition our request with a presumed answer. Do we really believe God will do what is best or do we just *say* we believe it?

Review God's promises and be willing to accept His wisdom.

In Matthew 6:30 God promises to supply our needs even better than He does nature's needs.

In Matthew 7:11 He promises:

a. Even as we earthly fathers_____

_____

b. God will _____

c. What is the prerequisite? _____

_____

That same prerequisite is mentioned in Philippians 4:6.

a. We are to be: _____

b. We are to ask God by: _____

   and_____ with_____

God asks but one additional thing from us if He is to answer (1 Thessalonians 5:18):

a. We are to *always:* _____

b. We can be sure that whatever happens it is:_____

_____

3. Establish the Minimum Testimony of God's Ownership.

    To "breathe" financially, it is important to establish a regular habit of giving. Those who have experienced the richness of God's freedom know that surrendering the *first* part to God was an essential step.

    Luke 6:38 has God's promise:

    a. If we give (out of love) then: _____

    _____

    b. What is God's measure? _____

    _____

    Put these principles into *practice* in your life:

    1—Surrender all ownership to God daily.

    2—Accept God's answers.

    3—Acknowledge God's ownership.

Applying God's Wisdom

In living by God's plan, it helps to have a list of principles to consider in making decisions. We are all faced with numerous opportunities that affect God's money. Left to our own logic and resources, Satan will dupe us into his traps. By analyzing *every* decision against God's principles, those snares *can* be avoided.

These are *principles* as opposed to *laws*. God gives them to enhance our lives because He understands what is best for us. Failure to follow His principles will result in financial loss and usually a loss of fellowship.

Discuss each of these principles with your group.

1. Avoid Speculation.

   Seek God's increase and avoid any speculation "schemes" or unethical involvements. Many times those programs are not only unethical, but also illegal. The result of a Christian's involvement will be a loss of witness, a loss of money, and a loss of credibility.

   Examples of such schemes are pyramid franchising, multilevel distributorships, unregistered stocks, promotional land ventures, and scores of other ventures.

   > "Do not weary yourself to gain riches, cease from your consideration of it. When you set your eyes on it, it is gone. For wealth certainly makes itself wings, like an eagle that flies toward the heavens" (Proverbs 23:4-5).

2. Keep Your Finances Current.

Never do anything that will jeopardize your financial freedom. That includes making purchases or investments. Do not depend on some future event (such as a raise or potential sale) to meet an obligation. *Sacrifice* your wants and desires if necessary, but do not overextend yourself.

> "For which one of you, when he wants to build a tower, does not first sit down and calculate the cost, to see if he has enough to complete it?" (Luke 14:28).

3. Do Not Go Into Debt to Do God's Work.

To launch out "on feeling"—without clear direction—and then realize that God's reputation will suffer if He doesn't provide the money, is tempting God and forcing His hand. Matthew 4:7 forbids that:

> "Jesus said to him, . . . It is written, 'You shall not tempt the Lord your God.' "

4. Give Rather Than Lend to the Needs of Others.

Although a loan to other Christians is scripturally sound, the result is too often a loss of friendship. An outright gift will be a testimony of your commitment and will often provide an opportunity for sharing.

> "Because of the proof given by this ministry they will glorify God for your obedience to your confession of the Gospel of Christ, and for the liberality of your contribution to them and to all" (2 Corinthians 9:13).

5. Avoid Co-signing for Anyone.

Co-signing is to pledge your assets against the debt of another. Scripture strictly forbids that wherever it speaks of "surety" and "striking hands" in the following references: Proverbs 6:1; 17:18; 20:16; and 27:13.

By co-signing you may encourage someone to borrow beyond his ability to repay.

> "A man of great anger shall bear the penalty, for if you rescue him, you will only have to do it again" (Proverbs 19:19).

6. Evaluate Purchases Based on Needs, Wants, Desires.

God has promised to provide for our needs, not our wants or desires. Many Christians are unhappy because they have not distinguished luxuries from necessities.

> "And if we have food and covering, with these we shall be content" (1 Timothy 6:8).

7. Never Make Financial Decisions under Pressure or in a Hurry.

The keynote of most phony schemes or inferior product sales is the necessity of a quick decision. Almost without exception pressured financial decisions are later regretted. Trust God's wisdom. If He is behind the transaction, there will be sufficient time to discern His direction.

> "And in your knowledge, self-control, and in your self-control, perseverence, and in your perseverence, godliness" (2 Peter 1:6).

8. Accept God's Decreases as Well as His Increases as Positive Direction.

Remember that God's perfect will may be best served by our need rather than our prosperity. To the Christian who is trusting Christ moment by moment, quality of life is *totally* independent of circumstances.

The ability to thank God in *every* circumstance demonstrates full dependence on Him, and the financial area is often used by God to develop our maturity.

> "I know how to get along with humble means, and I also know how to live in prosperity; in any and every circumstance I have learned the secret of being filled and going hungry, both of having abundance and suffering need. I can do all things through Him who strengthens me"
> (Philippians 4:12-13).

9. If You Don't Have Peace—*Don't Buy.*

Often we are not responsive to God's guidance because we become emotionally involved with an impending financial decision. As a last resort God will simply establish within us a feeling of uneasiness to stop our direction. The principle here is—if you don't have peace, don't get involved. Take the time to pray and think about it; perhaps God has some alternative provision for you.

> "It is the blessing of the LORD that makes rich, and He adds no sorrow to it"
> (Proverbs 10:22).

> "Rest in the LORD and wait patiently for Him" (Psalm 37:7a).

12

Practical Applications

"Commit your works to the LORD, and your plans will be established" (Proverbs 16:3).

Practical Applications

Information without application is useless. In this section you will find ideas to help you apply God's principles of finance.

Each area should be carefully and prayerfully considered and then applied. This section may be better used by filling out the plans as a family unit and then discussing the application in a group session.

Personal Communication Goals

Communication is vital to family financial planning. Included here are some questions for husbands and wives. It is suggested that each complete them separately. Answer them on a separate sheet of paper as if your spouse were asking each question. Then, without distractions, evaluate these together. Pray about them before you discuss your answers, and open your heart to the Holy Spirit.

These questions are meant to improve communication between partners who sincerely seek better understanding. They are not intended to become ammunition for couples with family problems.

Evaluate these as if your husband/wife were asking you:

1. What are your personal goals in life?

_____

_____

_____

2. What personal goals have you set for this coming year?

_____

_____

_____

3. How can I help you achieve your goals?

_____

_____

_____

4. What can I do to help or improve our financial situation?

_____

_____

5. Do you feel there is a proper balance between my outside activity and my time at home? _____

6. Would you like me to do more things around the house such as cleaning, decorating, etc.? _____

7. What would you consider as priorities in regard to my activities outside the home?

_____

_____

8. Do you feel I need to improve in the way I dress, my appearance, manner, attitudes?

_____

Marriage Goals

A result of putting Christ *first* in a marriage is not only *staying* together but *growing* together.

1. Do you believe that our marriage is maturing and that we are becoming closer?

   _____

2. Do you feel we clearly communicate with each other?

   _____

3. Do you feel that I am sensitive to your personal needs?

   _____

4. What would you like me to say or do the next time you seem to be angry with me or are not speaking to me?

   _____

5. The next time you are late in getting ready to go someplace, what would you like me to say or do?

   _____

6. What would you like me to do or say the next time you seem to be getting impatient with something or someone?

   _____

7. What would you like me to say or do if you begin to criticize someone?

_____

8. Do you feel I need to improve in getting ready on time or getting to meetings on time?

_____

9. Do you feel that we should go out together more often?

_____

10. Do I make cutting remarks about you or criticize you in front of other people?

_____

11. What should I do in public to encourage you?

_____

12. Do I respond to your suggestions and ideas as if I had already thought of them instead of thanking you and encouraging you to contribute more?

_____

13. Do I tell you enough about what I do every day?

_____

14. What little acts of love do I do for you? _____
_____

15. What do I do most often that angers you?
_____

16. Do I convey my admiration and respect often enough?
_____

17. Do we "play act" a happy marriage in front of other people?
_____

18. What do you think 1 Corinthians 7:3-7 means?
_____

19. What are the responsibilities of a "help-mate"?
_____
_____

20. Do we give each other the same attention as we did before we had children?
_____

Family Goals

As a Christian couple begins to establish family goals, it is necessary to understand the roles each member satisfies in God's plan.

GOD CALLS THE PLAYS... WE EXECUTE THE PLAN!

FAMILY GOALS

1. What are your family goals?

_____

_____

_____

2. Do you feel we are achieving them?

_____

3. a. (Wife) What can I do to help you fulfill your responsibilities as spiritual leader of our family?

_____

b. (Husband) How can I better fulfill my responsibilities as spiritual leader?

_____

_____

4. Do you feel we are meeting the spiritual needs of our family?

_____

5. What kinds of family devotions should we have?

_____

6. Do you feel we have a consistent prayer life together?

_____

7. List the responsibilities stated for the husband/wife in the following passages:

1 Peter 3:1-2 _____

Colossians 3:18-19_____

1 Timothy 2:11-15 _____

1 Corinthians 11:3 _____

Ephesians 5:17-33 _____

8. Do you feel we are adequately involved in our local church?

_____

9. Do you feel we are meeting the basic needs of our family?

_____

10. Should we improve our eating habits?

_____

11. Should we get more exercise?

_____

12. Do we make good use of our time? For example, do we watch too much TV? Should we have more hobbies? Read more?

_____

13. How and when shall we discipline our children? What do you think is the biblical viewpoint of discipline?

_____

14. Briefly note the responsibilities of parents and their children in the following passages:

Colossians 3:20-21_____

Hebrews 12:5-11 _____

Proverbs 3:11-12 _____

Ephesians 6:4 _____

15. What kind of instruction and training should we be giving our children in the home?

_____

_____

Family Financial Goals

By a conservative estimate at least 60-70 percent of the problems in a Christian home revolve around finances. Communication is the first step to finding God's cure.

1. Do you think I handle money properly?

   _____

2. How could I better manage our money?

   _____

   _____

3. Do you think I am:
   a. Too frugal? _____
   b. Too extravagant? _____
   c. About right? _____
   Why? _____

   _____

4. Do you think I accept financial responsibilities well?

   _____

5. Do you think we communicate financial goals well?

   _____

6. What is your immediate financial goal?

   _____

7. What is your primary goal for this year?

   _____

8. What is your plan for our children's education?

   _____

9. What is your retirement goal?

   _____

10. What do you think about tithing?
    a. Is it necessary?_____

    b. Where should it go? _____

11. How do you feel about *giving* in general?

    _____

12. Do you like the way we live?

_____

13. What changes would you like to see? _____

_____

_____